Poetry With My Love

To Carrie Jone Loftus

With my very
best wishes

Vance Trimble

Published by Poets of America Press,
a division of Market Tech Associates, Inc.
1304 Hilltop Avenue, Wilmington DE 19809

Poets of America Press books are available at special discounts for bulk purchases, sales promotion, fund raising, or educational purposes.

Manufactured in the United States of America

Library of Congress Cataloging-in-Publication Data
Trimble, Josie Crump, 1882–1940.
Poetry with my love / Josie Crump Trimble.—1st ed.
p. cm.
ISBN 0-9705399-5-9 (alk. paper)
I. Title.

PS3570.R517 P6 2000
811´.52—dc21

10 9 8 7 6 5 4 3 2 1

First Edition

POETRY WITH MY LOVE

Josie Crump TRIMBLE

POETS OF AMERICA PRESS

This book is dedicated to Josie Crump Trimble's daughter-in-law, Elzene Miller Trimble, and to Elzene's only child, Carol Ann Trimble Nordheimer. In a rare and lovely way, this poet's wonder and enjoyment of versifying was genuinely and equally shared by her "daughter" and this granddaughter.

My Mysterious Muse

Do not ask me why I say these things I write,
I cannot tell you. I do not know.
Sometimes I soar the clouds in my wild flight;
Sometimes the cloven hoof makes me walk slow,
My mind is not my own.
Generations, so very many, have fashioned it.
The whirlwind which they sowed, I reap.
I wonder, when to my judgment I must go,
Will all my forebears be there to plead
For me, or will they sleep and never know
My dire extremity, my desperate need?

Josie Crump Trimble

CONTENTS

BUBBLES

Bubbles

Bubbles are such useless things,
But they hold a rainbow bright.
They dance upon the air
Then vanish from our sight.

A little child, I loved to blow
Bright bubbles, light and fair.
And when they burst and vanished
I sought them everywhere.

My rhymes are like my bubbles—
Just froth, just bits of foam—
Yet, in my dreams my songs go forth
And bring my bubbles home.

Tomorrow

Give me one more kiss than yesterday,
Tomorrow means one day less in which to live.
I hate the hours that slip so speedily away;
Too soon today brings a tomorrow
When we must say our last goodbye.

A Sonnet to Age

Come make your home with me Old Age.
I fear you not, I greet you with delight.
This morning you lagged far behind;
The sun gone down, you walk with me tonight.
I welcome you. I find you pleasant,
You seem to know the wrong or right
Of everything. You have read Life's page,
Both sides of it. I rather like you, dear Old Age.
Long years ago I trembled at the sight
Of you and cried: "Please pass me by.
Youth is so sweet. Age, if you dare to come
I cannot live with you. I need must die."
But Youth was foolish. I find you sage.
Come tarry long with me, Old Age.

G. L. T., Beloved

Just let me live!
Let my life be full.
I'll take the sorrow
To find the pleasure sweet.
I'll strive and labor long
So I may enjoy my idle moments.
I'll bear the burden of a friendship lost
To prize the smiles of friends more true.
I'll drink my cup, wine, dregs, yes all
If God, if Life, will leave me you.

Your Gifts

You say, "I come to you with empty hands."
My sweet, the music of your dancing feet
Brings to my heart a lovely song.
You say, "I take and never give."
Your faith and love have made me wish to live.
Never say to me again, your hands of gifts are bare.
My dearest, dear, you gave me the smile I wear.

My Prayer

Lord, teach me consideration of others
Lest I take advantage of old age
To scold and insult young people.
Leave me memories of my own
Youthful indiscretions and waywardness
And remembering will give me patience.
Lord, let me keep the knowledge that young eyes
Cannot see the dirt in evil that comes
Only to us who have known much besmirching.
Lord, give me tolerance but let not tolerance
Grow into indifference.
Let my love for those I hold dear be undemanding.
Let me know always that:
Ambition is bitter, that love grows tired,
    that power becomes impotent,
      that gold is just a metal—but happiness
      is reborn whenever a child laughs.
It is carried on the rays of the sun.
Happiness comes with each Spring. It is found in the rainbow.
Happiness is free to every asking heart.
Dear Lord, whatever age shall take away, leave me happiness.
And when I grow old and tired, too tired to hold happiness,
    please let me die.

The Seasons

Gentle breezes,
Cool rains,
Brown earth,
Biological urge;
This is Spring.

Blue skies,
Growing things,
Fragrant blossoms,
Love's fruition;
This is Summer.

Frosty air,
Dry grass,
Tinted leaves,
Love wanes;
This is Autumn.

Gray skies,
Snow blanket,
Barren bleakness,
Love is dead;
This is Winter.

The Silver Ship

I have a little silver ship
Upon a glass sea blue.
I'm mariner of the Silver Ship,
My dreams make up the crew.

The passengers who sail
With us are never ill or sad,
No mutineers are with our crew,
The weather never bad.

I always steer a westerly course
When the voyage is but done
The Silver Ship clips waters blue
And sails into the sun.

Years and Years

When young, I carelessly spent the years,
It seemed there were so many.
The days were simply moments,
The years not worth a penny.

And now I hoard each precious year.
I find, since growing old,
The fleeting years are very few
And worth their weight in gold.

Aria Dolorosa

In my garden half-blown roses
Grew beside the graveled walk.
By the white fence in a corner
Stood a withered holly hock.

The blue sky o'er my garden
Darkened quickly with a rain.
And when the storm was over
And the sun shone bright, again

All the lovely half-blown roses
Were scattered petals on the walk.
By the white fence in a corner
Stood the withered holly hock.

Sounds

When dark is slowly creeping down
And lights are twinkling in the town
The sound that makes my heart most glad
Is the cheery whistle of my lad,
Far down the street.

No prima donna's clearest trill
Is half as fine as his whistle shrill
(Perhaps 'tis slightly off the key)
But it sounds true harmony for me.
It makes life sweet.

Then as my lad draws very near
It is not his whistle that I hear
(Although he is lilting like a lark)
So merrily ringing in the dark.
It is my heart's beat.

DREAMS

My Ozark Hills

All day long I scan the endless prairie.
It reaches East. It reaches West.
There is naught but endless plain and silver sky,
No hills to give my eyes some rest.

At night, when everything is still,
I watch the shadows in the moonlight
And make of every one a hill.

All green I see my hills; the tender grass of Spring
The green of Summer that makes a hazy blue.
And then I see my hills with Autumn gold bedecked
And trees, those lovely trees, of every shade and hue.

My dream goes with the moonlight,
Day brings back the prairie, mile on mile.
Night time brings my hills again;
They bring contentment, and I smile.

I Own The World

The whole wide world is mine.
The coldest mountain peak,
The bluest, deepest lake
Is mine. Is mine to take.
Glittering sunbeams, dripping rain,
Sandy desert, fertile plain, is mine.

The ocean's green with frosty crest,
I choose the thing that I like best,
The singing birds, the planes in air,
The gems, the treasures everywhere.
Fruits, food, power and pride are mine.

I own all upon which I look.
I simply have to choose my book.

Dreams

When I pass down the avenue
I sometimes window shop.
Perhaps people wonder,
As they look at
My wrinkled face and gray hair,
Why I stand before the sub-deb window.
They cannot know
That I am shopping
For the daughter I never had.

It's lots of fun to furnish her room,
To buy her pretty dresses and undies.
One day I pretended to promise
To ask her daddy for a new car;
But I scold myself for that.
No need for an old maid
To let her imagination carry her
Too far.

A Lovely Visitor

Spring came into my room today,
Her gown was tulip red.
I sensed a breeze so soft and sweet,
And the damp young grass beneath her feet.
My hungry heart cried, "Stay."
        *   *   *
Spring rustled the leaves of a weeping willow
And scattered daffodils over my pillow.

22

The Passing Silhouette

On winter mornings, when I wake
Before it is time to rise,
I look out of my window
With sleep be-fuddled eyes.

Against the cold, gray of the dawn
The scene I see is set,
And I pretend it is a play:
The Passing Silhouette.

A little figure, neat and trim
Goes tripping down the street,
Behind her is a husky shape
With clumsy, plodding feet.

A truck, which in the brilliant sun
Would shine with brass and paint,
Is just another Silhouette
Against the sky so faint.

Common things are strangely queer,
Shapes grotesque and shadows gay
Make up my Passing Silhouette
Until dawn flames into day.

As I Desire Me

You, Fates who spin, I ask one thing;
It's this: Give me the power to smile.
If hard luck hits me in the face
Let me breathe deep and have the grace
To say: "Luck changes after awhile."
If I should ever break an arm,
I'll be glad no harm befell the other.
No matter what the years may bring
I want to smile through tears that sting.
Then, when I crack this earthly skin,
I'll be a jolly Cherubim.

Loveliest Things

A hillside dressed in grasses green
Trimmed with buttons of gray rock
With violets on its shoulder
An elm tree pressed against a cold blue sky
A twisted path through a wooded glen
Green ferns on a mossy boulder
An elderberry's lacy bloom
A white curtain swaying in a room
And a wood fire, when I'm older.

Horoscope

1.

This for you is a year of change
Many short journeys in places strange.
Comfort will come to you, when old;
Beware at this time to guard against cold.

2.

When you're in the dumps be not dismayed
At the last moment you will get aid.
Matrimony is clearly indicated
Beware of heart strain or you'll get pixilated.

3.

This year you will fall heir to wealth
And you should take great care of your health.
If you should quarrel with your friends
Shun disappointment and make amends.

4.

This will be a year of trouble and woe,
Changes and journeys, a short distance you'll go.
Business will trouble but be of good cheer
Success will attend you. You'll find it next year.

5.

Across the ocean you will go,
Perhaps to see the King,
But don't put on an eager show,
It won't get you anything.

Sacrifice Supreme

All my life I have had a dream
That sometime I would make
The sacrifice supreme.
Such as:
Rescuing from a burning building
A crippled lady, old and sweet,
And then
With a sad, brave smile
I would nobly expire upon a crowded street.
Or—
Thrust my way through an angry mob
And save a man from sudden death
While
The bullet meant for him
Pierced my heart. And with my dying breath
I'd smile and say, "Forgive them, Lord."
I have even visioned this tragic scene:
My broken, lifeless body spread upon the village green.
There
Cuddled in my arms
The mangy, little cur I'd saved from harm.
* * *
This morning while bathing the baby
I was frightened by a mouse.
I left the child in the bathtub
And fled madly from the house.

Green Thumb?

I do so want a garden
A lovely fragrant garden
Where grow daisies, hollyhocks, and rue.
I try to make a garden
But just weeds grow.
I never get a flower in my garden
No matter what I do.

A Vanished Dream

I had the dearest little dream
I nurtured it with care
I held it close against my heart
We were a happy pair!
My heart grew cold within my breast
I thrust my dream aside
And now, I have no happiness
My little dream has died.

Nirvana

If for me there is no dreamless sleep
And once again my soul must creep
Its weary way to reach perfection,
I'd like to be a scarlet butterfly
In slanting rays of sunshine.

As if in human form I must be
I choose this state of bliss for me:
Blue grass 'neath an apple tree
The grass my bed
Spring sky for my canopy
Sweet-smelling petals dropping
Gently on my head.

Gray Concourse

There is a curving gray street,
It is made of concrete.
It has an elm tree at the bend;
I long so to see beyond the elm tree,
To follow this street to the end.

My feet never stray
This intriguing way,
My heart and my eyes make the quest
Of this curving gray street
That is made of concrete
And the elm at the bend that turns west.

Farewell

If I can dry
My tear-wet eye
And show a smile
I'll say, "Goodbye."
If I can choke my sorrow down
And just be glad, for the other town,
I'll say, "Goodbye."

You have been my friend
My whole life long.
My heart is heavy,
My grief is strong.
And I—well—I
Just can't say, "Goodbye."

Futility

I do so long to write a poem,
Not one that is classic or profound.
I want to write of love that knows no ending,
Of mothers, babies, tillers of the ground.
If I could write the feel of early morning
Or print the glory of the sunset sky
And tell the joy that comes with faith aborning,
But this is not to be; I only try.

Sunbeams and Shadows

Tiny green leaves from a planted seed,
The earthy tang of an uprooted weed,
A dandelion, snug, like an egg in a nest,
A coquetting breeze coming out of the west.
Simple things these, but I hold them dear,
For the Winter is done and Spring is here.

Peach blossoms on boughs brown and sturdy
Danced to the tune of Spring's hurdy-gurdy.
The grass made a carpet where shadows played,
The sunbeams laughed in the elm tree's shade.
The rain-washed earth was fresh and new.
I alone was sad, for I thought of you.

Sunsets

If it were not for sunsets
What would poets do?
I want to write of sunsets
Of skies all gold and blue.
When the sun sinks brightly
I can almost hear it say:
"Treat the darkness lightly,
I'll bring another day."

What I Like

I like women short and small,
I like men folks big and tall.
I don't like babies when they squall
But me, I dearly love the Fall.

Spring is O.K. with tender green,
Summer's grand with silver sheen
But give me the Harvest Queen;
It's Fall, I mean.

I can't write an eulogy
'Bout things I smell or things I see.
I can't describe a golden tree
With frosted leaves, but it's Fall for me.

After The Flower Show

Why did I choose you
When hundreds of roses
Flaunted their beauty?
There were so many
Wonderful flowers,
All so enchanting.
Why did I choose you?

The roses about you
Looked pale, fragile, forlorn,
While your crimson beauty
Was gorgeous, sweet scented,
Dew-kissed by the morn.

I wanted to hold you
But pity o'ercame me
And you couldn't blame me.
My touch would blacken your crimson,
Spoil your fragrance rare.
With lingering look and loving glance,
Smiling, I left you there.

The Optimist

Each morning finds me breathless
With out-stretched hands
To grasp a long expected happiness.
The setting sun, forerunner of the night,
Promises with each golden ray
That I shall rise tomorrow
To find another perfect day.

The Pessimist

Another day, Oh, gosh!
Twelve long hours of pish and posh,
Technocracy, work, and woe.
Time doesn't fly; Time is slow.

Sundown, I can't sleep.
Twelve darkened hours to slowly creep.
Burning eyelids, tired and sad.
Tomorrow will be just as bad.

PROGENY

Longing

Just a pair of trusting eyes
Looking into mine.
A pair of little grubby hands
Playing with a kite.
A pile of nails or wad of string
Lying on the floor.
To think: it used to worry me.
It wouldn't any more.

The house is all so very neat
And very quiet too.
Nobody slams the kitchen door
The way he used to do.
Nobody wakes me up at dawn.
Nobody skins his toe.
To think: I used to quarrel
But now I miss him so.

My heart is ever longing
For a pair of trusting eyes
And only in my dreams I hold
A chubby little hand.
To think: I used to scold him.
The child has grown to manhood
And I am old and lonely for the lad
I loved but didn't understand.

To A Baby's Cup

Poor little cup, you have been empty so long.
Your bright gold lining,
And the silver, too, is almost black.
Come, little cup, I will make you shine again.
You shall have your brightness back.

All your dents are dear to me. I see
His impatient baby hands
Beating you upon the tray
Of his high chair.
Years ago I put you away;
His need of you was done.

Now I am like you,
Dear little cup.
I am full of dents and tarnished
And Time has robbed me of my son.

Play Acting

Hey! Big feller, don't I look tough?
    See the sharp spur on my boot,
Chaps long and hairy protecting my legs.
    Look out thar now, or I'll shoot!

Women and children I leave on the trail
    While ole hoss and I ride hell for leather.
Outlaw nor sheriff can't ketch us at all
    If ole hoss and I stick together.

Why, daddy, you're skeered! It's only a joke
    I'm just playin'. Of course, I won't shoot.
It's my birthday, I'm nine. I guess you forgot
    'Bout givin' me this cowboy suit.

Peace

The radio is silent. The games are on the shelf.
No magazines nor books are on the floor.
The football in un-flated and the glass it broke
Has been replaced in the front door.

I brush my hair and find it somewhat gray
And wrinkles, too, have marked my placid brow.
I seek my room and find it quiet now.
My work-worn hands I fold upon my breast.
The children are in school. Holidays are o'er
And I, a tired mother, in peace shall rest.

Johnny Expresses Himself

Gee! but I'm hungry and my overalls need patchin'.
Dad says he's gotten tired of this eternal batchin'.
We used to have the most to eat
Our house was always clean and neat
But now, we hustle for our grub
Since Mother joined the Writers Club.

She sits all day with pen and ink
She tries so very hard to think
Up rhymes to bring her fame.
I'm so lonesome! Ma ain't the same.

She never makes us cakes and pies;
She sits around with staring eyes
And says the Muse she's seeking.
But I ain't never seen that thing
And I've done a lot of peeking.

Now I like poems, I do, the kind that's in a book.
But I wish Ma would settle down
And clean the house, and cook.

She cooks so awful good
Her biscuits taste like more.
But if you ask me the question
Her poems? Gosh! They're pore.

Dad says what Ma needs is soap,
A washboard and a tub.
But Ma is mighty happy
Since she joined the Writers Club.

He Doesn't Do It Now

Out in the Autumn wood
  He sought the trees where wild grapes clustered
And garnered all that he could carry home.
  My yeast and sugar filled a box of tin
The juice from all the grapes was then poured in.

Next morning came. I sought my loaf of bread
  But found the box with foaming wine instead.
Down kitchen drain the juice we had to pour.
  I thought: "Wine brewing days are o'er."

Yet soon again he sought the village wood
  And found again the wild grapes growing good.
Another mash was quickly made,
  Enclosed in fruit jars and buried with a spade
Beneath the ground.

This juice would ripen, then grow old
  To cheer the heart of my son John, so bold.
Again the juice went back from whence it came,
  It ran out o'er the top.
Then, methought: "This time I'm sure he'll stop."

Last Saturday, once more, the wood he roamed
  And sought the vine and berry.
Again he tried to make some wine
  Once more contrary
To his desire, the juice remained quite sweet;
  The taste was puckery and gritty, too,
'Twas not the vintage to taste like Mountain Dew.

At last I breathe a prayer of thanks;
    Wine brewing days are done.
He has a new pup and a 'possum
    Has John, my youngest son.

Q. and A.

Little boy, little boy, have you any name?
Yes, sir, Yes, sir, 'n I'll be asking you the same.
My name is Danny Nanny. Very pretty, too.
Now, Mister, I'll be saying: What is the name of you?

To Vance

My songs I thought unsung
(I could not put them into words)
Are sung for me by you, my boy.
My dumb soul has come to life
In you, and this greater joy:
I read my dreams in what you write.

JITTERY JINGLES

Life

She was a modern maid,
The youth was modern, too.
They both called a spade, a spade,
No other name would do.
Sentiment was all the bunk,
Love a biological call.
Lares and penates a lot of junk,
Realism was the life for all.
The maid plied her lipstick,
The lad rubbed his tiny mustache.
Mascara darkened her eyelids thick,
He felt in his pocket for cash.
The orchestra played a jazzy tune,
They swayed to the music together,
Forgot if it was morning or noon,
They gave no heed to the weather.

  * * *

The maid is washing her dishes.
The youth, cheerful and debonair,
Is lifting their laughing baby
Out of his new high chair.

Nudism. Yes and No

To swim and dive, I would admire
To hit the water without attire;
But, were I to a-hunting go,
I would not choose the nude. No, no!

Somehow to scratch my back or knee
On brier or weed don't appeal to me.

When dancing on a sunlit beach
Or playing in the rain,
A tiger skin or a swimming suit
Would glorify this Jane.

It is not because I am a prude,
But I'd be a wall flower in the nude.

I would not choose fig leaves
To adorn me here and there;
I'd gladly shuck my dress and shoes
But I must keep my brassiere.

My Past

Dear God! My past came back to me today.
My conscience suffered. I tore my hair.
I crossed myself, and said a prayer.
I saw a dress, my God!
Like one I used to wear.

Jits and Jots

Just to be healthy, alive and awake
Is like having a slice of birthday cake.

A corn on my toe nearly drives me mad
And I think this last one is the worst I have had.

The abundance of my garden my expectations exceed.
Very few flowers—an abundance of weed.

In Winter one dreams of days warm and sunny;
When the weather is hot we want ice. Aren't we funny?

Young people who pick flaws with the whole universe
Grow into cranky old folks who think the world's growing worse.

Some things that are forever new:
Love, the weather, first babies
And the things that I do.

If I could make a lovely rose,
A rose without a thorn,
I bet the florists would be glad
For the day that I was born.

I used to want to be an angel
Way up in the sky.
Now I wish I owned an airplane
That I knew how to fly.

Once I craved much gold and gear,
A tiara for my head.
Now, I'm content with three square meals
And some covers for my bed.

Don't sit around and curse your luck,
Buy an accident policy and meet an oil truck.

The world's a lovely place when e're the dawn appears,
But don't forget one night to God
For you is a thousand years.

Woe Begone

I'm so doggone tired trying to smile
When my pocketbook is flat
And more than that
My jaws are cramped from grinning all the while.

I don't want to be a martyr, or a saint
I'm tired pretending what I ain't.
I'm broke. I'm bare and needy.
My hose are full of runners
And all my clothes look seedy.
    *   *   *
Ho hum! My raving is a jest
I'm always smiling, always jolly.

Moon Mist

The moonlight made a fluffy soft mist.
The shadowed peach blooms were pale amethyst,
The hyacinths, white, were ghostly and pale
And the tulip heads bent from stems, slender and frail.
The jonquils, too, sun-colored and sturdy,
Were quietly waiting for Spring's hurdy-gurdy.
A saucy young breeze brought a rollicking tune
And the flowers all danced in the mist of the moon.

Red Versus White

Spring is here and I confess
My innards feel a great distress.
Corpuscles red, Corpuscles white
Are skipping around in great delight.

If I do not mistake their meaning
I think they are doing their Spring cleaning.

I wish they would not scratch and bite,
There is room for both if they act right.
One cries, the germs must go,
The other says: "Nay, nay, no, no."

No matter how I moan and squirm
They squabble o'er each little germ.
But I know this, if they would quit
Then I could sleep a little bit.

She

Call me a baggage, a bum, or a cow,
I'm not easily affronted. But anyhow
Call me some name. The thing that irks me
Is just to be called generically She.

When I Am Dead

When I have crossed the bar,
If I slip through the gate that stands ajar,
I'd like to trip along the golden way
And have St. Peter smile at me and say:
"One wish to you I'll grant."
There will be no hesitation on my part
For I will answer, with a grateful heart,
"Give me those clippings I have stuck around
For which I've madly searched, but never found."

My Garden

The riotous morning glory
Clambers my garden wall.
A white trellis is ruddy with roses
And a sunflower towers o'er all.

The clove pink vies its fragrance
With the mignonettes sweet lavender bloom.
A scarlet cascade of verbenas
Brightens an evergreen's gloom.

These are my flowers by day.
Although darkness obscures my sight
I am happy because I remember
And dream of my garden at night.

Heat Waves

The brazen bowl of a summer sky
Touches the dry, hot grass upon the hill.
The trees with withered branches are drooping.
The birds and other flying things are still.

I would that I were a chemist, wise,
And had the power to make some weather.
I would mix a heavy winter snow
And the Summer sun together.
Gosh! Ain't it hot?

Nancy Explains

Daddy is an Injun
I am Injun, too.
Mother is a white girl
'Ist like you.

Paleface is a nice girl,
She stays here. You see
She loves big Injun daddy
And little Injun me.

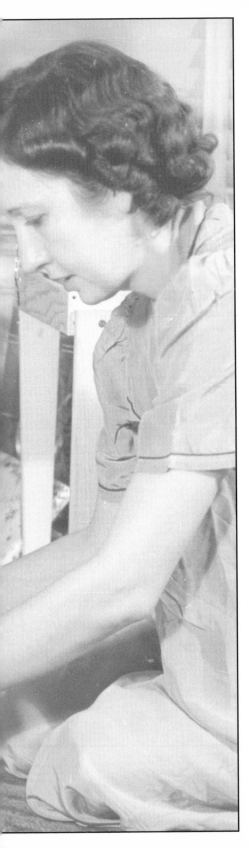

YULETIDE

A Christmas Prayer

Dear Lord of All, cease counting sparrows as they fall.
Please let the hairs of permanent waves remain un-numbered.
This Christmas give Thy angels one thing to do,
From other things let them be un-encumbered.
Thy little son lay in a manger, but he was safe
And warm. Wise men brought him gifts. Angels smiled.
While on this earth, Christ loved each little child.
Because of this, I make my prayer. 'Way off up there
In Heaven, you may not know that many babies
Have no beds in which to lay their bodies, blue and cold,
Their little faces, pinched by hunger, look so old.
No good Wise men bring gifts to them on Christmas night.
I humbly pray: for Christ's sake make things right,
Let every child be clothed and fed,
Let every stocking hold a toy.
And give no mother any cause a tear to shed.
If you remember me, you know I seldom pray
But this I ask with all the strength of my poor soul,
Let thine own little ones be happy, Christmas day.

A Christmas Letter

I've dressed a small girl's dolly. And I've made the doll a hat. I've bought a baby's rattle and a cunning rubber cat. I've strung long strings of popcorn. And I have a gun that shoots. There's a fruit cake in the pantry. For John, I have some boots.

I went to Mr. Kresse's and got a game or two, but, in looking through my bundles there is not one thing for you. I didn't overlook it. I think of you each day, as one of the very dearest friends who has ever come my way. I've made the same excuses a dozen years, it seems. You see I'm short on money. Nobody sells gifts for dreams.

So that is why this letter is coming straight to you. May the coming year bring sunshine, and your dearest wish come true. By just adding that I love you, I will close this Christmas letter with a very hopeful promise that next year I may do better.

Christmas Verses

I would like to send a card to you
With something clever and something new
But, as you know, I'm not too bright
So I will send greetings, sweet but trite—
A merry, merry Christmas!

I'm busy
Hanging up a green wreath
Tying on a red bow
Shining up my dishes
And sending Christmas wishes.

You are there and I am here
It seems so far away—
But distance doesn't matter
Altho we are apart
I can wish you Merry Xmas
From the bottom of my heart.

Same as last year
Same as year before
Same as next year
Same for many more:
Merry Christmas!

I am fifty and fat, as everyone knows,
And I'd be a bum gift wrapped in holly and bows.
But, after all, I see no cause
Why I can't come with Santa Claus
And wish you a Merry Christmas.

Mistletoe is everywhere,
Xmas wreaths are hanging high,
Fir and cedar scent the air.
I smile, then softly sigh.
The gift I want I can not get
In my stocking or my shoe
Nor St. Nick put it in his pack.
The gift I want is—you.

Mistletoe is white,
Holly is red
Christmas is here
I wish I was dead.
    P.S.
    That was just to make a rhyme
    Life is a jolly game.
    I'm happy with the Yuletide
    And hope you are the same.

Christmas 1913

Dear Nannie:

I ordered you some oysters and then I happened to think you do not care for shell fish. So I ordered you something to drink. I ordered you champagne with bubbles floating light. Then I remembered that you do not drink, that you wear a ribbon white.

I rushed to buy a travelling bag, but when that thing got here, it didn't have your monogram, so it wouldn't do, my dear.

By this time I was desperate. So I drew on the bank for money. I simply can't understand cashiers. They certainly do act funny.

He talked about "accounts" and such, and threatened "the law" to beat the Dutch. I don't care for myself, of course, but disappointment surely follows for he knocked you out of a present from me when he turned down that million dollars.

Lovingly,
Babykins
(Josie C. Trimble)

Aftermath

Christmas tree is over
    Dinner eaten, too
Mother sitting idle
    Nothing else to do.

Brother's gone a-courting
    Sister, too, I guess.
Mother sits a-rocking
    Looking at the mess.

Daddy sorter dizzy
    Full of Christmas cheer
Mother keeps a-rocking
    Never seems to keer.

Buddy has a broken skate
    Sister's lost her map
Mother sits a-dreaming
    Sure enjoys her nap.

Suddenly wailing fills the air
    Baby is awake
Mother gets the castor oil
    For baby's stomach ache.

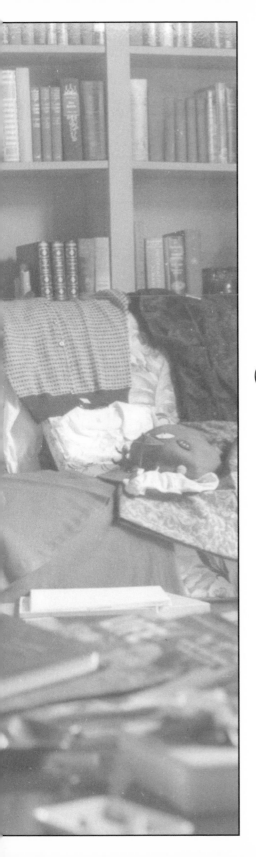

MEMORIES

Lonesome

I sometimes think I cannot wait to tell you
The many little things I see and hear,
The days have never seemed so long or lonely
And it is just because I miss you, dear.

I smile and try to pass the moments
With wildest fun or cheery bits of song,
And to the world I seem as happy
As when you lingered with us, weak, yet strong.

I can't tell anyone how much I miss you;
In fact, I only hope they do not know.
Yet, I would give the world to only kiss you,
To be your baby girl of long ago.

I would not call you back to share my sorrow,
I could not bear to see you suffer pain.
Still, I do wish you could be here this morning,
Your flowers look so sweet, since last night's rain.

Spring, I Think

If I could find an old house I know
I would open a white picket gate
And walk down the path where crocus grow
And the lilacs and hyacinths wait.

If I could stop at a windlassed well
And draw me a cool sweet drink
And hear the sound of your laughing voice
I would know it was Spring, I think.

October Church

The old witch rides upon her broom
The black cats are about
Ghosts, too, are standing in the gloom
Look out, Look out, you folks. Look out!
Remember this is just the time
When pumpkins all have faces
And it's the time for shoes and strings
In the very queerest places.

A Rose, Very Red

It is Mother's Day and I should wear
A fragrant, white carnation.
But for this custom I do not care,
It does not suit my inclination.

I much prefer a rose, a perfect rose,
Sweet scented, velvety and very red,
Upon a strong green stem. I suppose
The reason is, I never think of you as dead.

Your soul, proud, tender, and un-dismayed,
Brings consolation for each changing hour
And since your spirit does not fade
I choose a vivid living flower.

A La Emily Post

Children small have bottles
In bed; because they are not able
To sit up good and eat their food
From bowls upon a table.

Silver Goblet

Upon the table, by my bed, you stand
Graceful and shining. Precious
Because of hands, long dead,
Which grasped your slender stem.
And, yet, the luster that once shone
With the reflected glory of prismed
Candelabra, gives forth no rays
To light my darkening room.

Empty, too, of that sparkling wine
Which gives a zest to appetite,
And this is well, for hunger
Needs no stimulation.
The dancing flames from hearth fires
Of the long ago, made you warm
And golden. Now, when I touch you
With hands, stiff and blue, I find you cold.

Mother

I have heard songs about Mother,
I have read poems, too,
And it seems they have all
Been written to you.

For there is naught of loveliness, written or said,
That the glory of it doesn't rest on your head.
Just read all the songs and poems most divine,
And they'll be for you, dear Mother of mine.

My Flower

In snow-white lilies, sweet and fair,
I see my mother's lovely hair.
Violets are the shadows beneath her eyes,
Which were forget-me-nots, blue as the skies.
Lilacs are the smiles that lit her face.
Sweet flowers, from you I turn away,
Upon my breast I wear a bleeding heart, today.

Valentines

To Josephine

Once again I believe in Kris Kringle,
And I know fairies dance on my lawn,
I read you a Mother Goose jingle,
My wond'rings and doubtings are gone.

I cuddle you close on my shoulder,
My world-weary heart has its thrills.
Your soft, dimpled hands hold a surcease
For all of my cares and my ills.

Your innocent eyes bring me hope—
That someday my dreams will come true.
My life is better and sweeter
Because there's a baby like you.

To Margaret

My heart goes pitty pat
When e're I think of you.
And, if I were a kitty cat,
I could purr and purr for you.

Today and Yesterday

It is Mother's Day, for young mothers
A busy, long and tiring day
Caring for soft, young babies
With sweet red lips that laugh and fret.
There are dirty little hands to scrub, hurts to pet.

    *   *   *

Old mothers have their memories,
A tiny dress, a half-worn shoe
With rosemary for remembrance
Tied by a tiny ribbon, with a sprig of rue.

A Precious Day

     Hanging up towels is a tired woman
with a smudge of flour on her nose,
a burn on her elbow and her hair hanging
limply down about her moist face.
     This is the little woman—the keeper
of the house—the home-maker. And again
I ask you, what day is it? What big day?
What eventful, happy occasion?
Everybody knows, of course.
It's Mother's Day.

Elzene at Twenty

A Miss you have been on birthdays aplenty
But you were never a Missus until you were twenty.
And now comes the big thought, how shall I address you
When I say Happy Birthday
And whisper God bless you?
Of course there is Callie, but you say that is out.
I could say, "Mrs. Trimble, I am happy to shout
Congratulations! On this happy occasion."
But your aversion to that causes me this evasion.
There's Miller, Elzene, Elziner and dear—
All suitable names for your twentieth year.
But thinking it over, the name I like best
Is: My little daughter. For mixed up with the rest
Of this big bunch of menfolk I like a few girls
With sweet dainty manners
And permanent curls.
May your years be many, your happiness long
And this, little daughter, is the end of my song.

Lulu Vance Scott

What shall I say to a lady
Who is blankety-blank years young?
Shall I say I think it will be fine
When you celebrate your birthday at ninety and nine?
After all what a mess it would make
To set 99 candles on one birthday cake.

I could wish you a warm fireside
And a nice big easy chair
And, yet, with nothing to do,
You wouldn't be happy just sitting there.

Perhaps the wish that I would make
Would be something you wouldn't want or take.
So, I'm just sending word to you: You make your own wish.
Then, after you have done your part
I'll hold the wish safely in my heart
And whatever you want for whatever thrill
We will get for you--if you are living still
When you are one hundred and fifty.

What Kids Eat

In these days of sweat and blisters,
Nervous Misses and irritable Misters,
I hate to contact dull people and unpleasant topics
And the worst of all are mother myopics
Who look down their noses
While they talk about these and thoses
Their kids won't eat.
Johnny won't eat pork and beans,
Sister doesn't like spinach greens.
Such a noisy fuss they make;
If their brats won't eat bread, give 'em cake.
Mothers who discuss kids and tantrums
Should have abcesses in their anthrums.

She Slays Them

There was a fat man named Shorty
He married a widow, age forty.
They quarreled and fought
When they hadn't to ought.
Now she's the widow of Shorty.

SCRAPBOOK

Toll

Sometimes when I am gay with laughter
I have a subtle sense of fear
Which whispers that I may be sad
As toll to happiness
For all the joy I've had.

If to happiness I must pay toll
I want no wisp of pleasure,
Of merriment, the weak man's dole,
Not just a day of pain and care.

I want a heart filled to bursting
With joy and mirth.
Then bend me down with sorrow
And even as I pay my toll
I shall feel sure that happiness
Will come again tomorrow.

Vacation Suggestions

A quiet wood all cool and green
    And free from bugs, is nice, I ween.
A grassy bank, a gurgling brook
    A big fat worm upon a hook
Would be a very pleasing sight
    If the darned fish would ever bite.

A book of verse beneath a bough
    If the ant hill ants didn't sting, and how!
An evening drive in a motor car
    On a lonely road out rather far
A pop, a puncture, then a flat
    And the joy from the joy ride is out of that.
To swim in a pool is a happy thought
    Till you hang on a nail where your swim suit's caught.

A palm leaf fan, a tall cool drink,
    A whiff of joke makes you stop and think
It can't be done. You give a sigh
    Just another pleasure passing by.
To go on a train to visit mother
    The kids will catch one disease or another.
Tarry at home or gypsy around,
    The only safe place is a hole in the ground.

I'm Embarrassed

Do you know something? No doubt you do. But I'm embarrassed.

I have never given a great lot of thought to setting the world right or telling everybody how, but I suppose I have been satisfied with my own conclusions else why would I be in this state of upheaval? (I am not sure that I am spelling upheaval correctly.) This insecurity is getting me down.

The first thing wrong with me is that I love jigsaw puzzles. I can sit for hours and fit and refit small curlicue pieces of composition board or wood. I can sit while bread burns or the clock says noon. I can play with jigsaw and look with resentment when some tiresome person comes in to tell me the same thing twice. And yet I can gladly leave dear, darling jigsaw to embrace, figuratively or literally, some delightful friend and jiggy ceases to count until the departure of my friend makes desolate the hours. Then once again I'm a jigsaw fiend.

Something else is wrong with me. I love games of chance. Anything from a crap game to a Kentucky Derby thrills me. As my older brother once remarked, our family excels at sitting down games. And of all sitting down games I adore Bridge. Bridge, that reserved Pray do Bridge, Lily and Tiger Bridge, Auction and Contract. I do not play for social contact and I do not care to play by rules that Mrs. So-and-So says they use in Tulsa. I want to read and play by rules that are standard for the United States at least. But when people suggest Bridge is a waste of time and almost sinful, I feel embarrassed. I'm perturbed.

I wrote an article. The dear Lord knows I didn't "want ta." When I read it to my most dearly beloved unrelated, she said I was wrong. No harm in telling me that; we always grant each other the right to her personal opinion. And while I know she knows more in ten minutes about music than I ever will and she is a better critic of literature than I am—I'm queer, or maybe stubborn. God grant I admit being stupid —I stick to my own opinion—and by gad, my crippled, little deformed brain-child, begotten by force of the Study Club Programme Committee spawned by me, unwilling, unlettered me, is mine and I'm standing by the brat. I believe in her. But I'm embarrassed.

Then there is pronunciation. I'm scared. I used to say isolation or *isolation*. I've forgotten which, but whichever it was, is wrong. Then there's un-re-quited. I heard a lady say "*un-re-quited* love." I was afraid to laugh; I didn't know whether it was a joke or not. I just smiled a sad smile like I had an *un-re-quited* love. I'm afraid I'm ignorant. I'm perturbed.

Another awful thing. I'm not full of maternal love. I was crazy about my little helpless babies, but big children are just folks. I wish them well 'n everything but I like the man I'm living with better. I'm embarrassed. I'm not normal.

I couldn't and I wouldn't make a patch-work quilt, an embroidered quilt or knit a sweater suit for less than a million dollars and I couldn't get anyone to pay me five cents a hundred pounds for my handi-work. I'm not capable. I'm perturbed.

I really love to cook and wash dishes, but that is all. My idea of Heaven is a personal maid to stoop down and hang up my clothes. And here I am not one cent in the bank, just a forgotten woman. I'm lazy. I'm embarrassed.

When some people get angry they kick the dog or a chair. When I'm embarrassed I talk loud, disagree and feel helpless. Why is it wrong to think your own thoughts, act your own normal or abnormal way? I'm asking you in a loud voice because I'm embarrassed. I'm perturbed.

Villanelle

I never wrote a villanelle,
The Frenchman's old, poetic vice,
But, after all, it's just as well.

If I had anything to tell
In rhyme, I would think twice
Before I wrote a villanelle.

I know that I am dumb as hell
(Although the expression is not nice)
But, after all, it's just as well.

I might rob banks or toll a bell
Or even write love-lorn advice,
But I never wrote a villanelle.

I'm sure the poem would not sell
And, since it would not bring a price,
Why, after all, it's just as well.

While Limburger cheese retains its smell
The cats may whisper to the mice,
"She never wrote a villanelle
But, after all, it's just as well."

Advice to Junior High

Don't shoot paper wads
And don't scrape your feet.
Don't bring gum and candy to eat.
Don't slump down with your feet in the aisle
And don't look around at somebody and smile.
Don't whisper. Don't shout.
Don't wiggle about.
Don't stamp through the hall
When school has turned out.
Don't dispute with your teacher.
Don't blot your paper,
Don't try to be smart
And cut a new caper.
Don't be absent or late,
Don't make below A.
Don't pull some girl's hair
And "Teacher's pet" say.
Don't listen to me
Or the Don'ts I have given.
No pupil could do it
Unless he were in Heaven.

Verses for Cards

Green vines whispering at my window
Summer sunlight glinting through
Fragrances from sweet May roses
Always make me think of you.

Tears today mean smiles tomorrow,
Happiness follows every sorrow.
The clouds can't always drip with rain,
The sun will shine. You'll be happy again.

Like Humpty-Dumpty you burst your shell.
The king's men and his horses can't make you well.
But the surgeon's knife and a stitch or two
Will mend your shell till you're good as new.

Happy Birthday

I wish you a happy birthday,
I am sure you are feeling fine.
And, please keep celebrating
Till the candles on your birthday cake
Number ninety and nine.

After Your Operation

I am sure there's a smile on your face
And your chin is sticking out
And you haven't a care or a pain
Worth fussing about.

To a Young Mother

You have a sweet baby, I hear.
Please let me whisper in your ear,
I love that baby, pink and new,
But most of all I'm loving you.

SHADOWS

An Amateur Courts The Muse

To court the Muse
Is my excuse
For leaving the city's heat.
And I give no heed
To mortal need
As I sit in this cool retreat.

Two shimmery skies
Befool my eyes
And as I make inspection
I wonder if
I'm in a tiff
Or, is one sky a reflection?

If I should try
To kick the sky,
As I know I hadn't orter,
Now would I
Really hit the sky
Or step into the water?

The breath of air
That stirs my hair
Is supposed to be a zephyr
And yet, I fear
From the sniff I hear
It's only a Jersey heifer.

The greensward isn't green at all,
It's just a dusty brown.
The water isn't rippling,
It doesn't make a sound of any sort,
And I can't find a Muse to court.

The Muse is not behind a tree
Nor dancing in the shady wood.
She is nowhere
And I don't care.
I wouldn't court her if I could.

I'm not going to sigh and pine
(For what isn't mine).
A Muse I cannot get
I never will regret.
Shucks! For her sake I wouldn't
Give the nectar of the gods no odds
In exchange for a nice big juicy steak.

Shadows

I love the twilight
The time when day covers her blond beauty
With a soft mantle of gray
And slips away to meet the night.

'Tis then I wander
Out into my garden and sit beside a pool
And wait for you
To come. You always do.

I never look about.
I watch the shadow trees from whence you came;
I see you through their maze.
Kind shadows, dear shadows, stay with me
All my days.

A Still Small Voice

Yesterday was rainy and cold
A woman knocked at my door.
Her blue eyes were shadowed,
She looked tired and old.
She smiled and timidly said,
"Could I interest you in a Bible lecture?
You will find it the best you've ever read."

"I'm busy and I can't be bothered today."
My voice was cold as the rain,
I shut the door and turned her away.
I shall never see her again.
My fire was warm—the room cozy and bright
While she walked in the rain, weary and cold.
And I—I didn't rest well last night.

Our Mother

The gentle rain which falls in Springtime
And gives life to the tender grass and flowers
Is like the gentle, loving hands
Of that sweet mother of ours.

When lightning streaks across the sky
And the thundering storm clouds roll
We always think of mother
And the grandeur of her soul.

When the brightness of the morning sun
Makes all the world to shine
It is like mother's smile of welcome
Which makes her face to shine.

In evening when the sky is filled with sunset glow
And God's glory fills our hearts with peace
'Tis then we bow our heads and know
It is mother's benediction.

The Wraith

She came and stood beside my bed one night
  This silent woman in a robe of white
And through her body I could see
  My mirror which reflected me
But not my visitor so thin and light.

Why have you come, I said, why are you here?
  She only smiled at me. Her eyes were sweet and clear.
'Twas then that I knew that I would die,
  My loved ones I would tell goodbye
And with my white-robed woman I have no fear.
  * * *
She told us this, our sister good and sweet,
  And when she lay in her last sleep
A misty, frosty shape beside her coffin stood.

Smiling Through

You, Fates who spin, I ask one thing of you
It's this: give me the power to smile.
If hard luck hits me in the face
Let me breathe deep and have the grace
To say: "Luck changes after while."
If I fall down and break an arm
Let me just grin and say: "No harm
Befell the other."
No matter what the years may bring
I want to smile through tears that sting
Then afterwhile at Death I'll smile
And say, Hello, Life's brother!

A Nocturne

Softly, slowly creeping
You come while I lie sleeping.
Your long black robe of crepe
Brushes my eyelids and I wake.
As I look into the darkened space
I feel the breath of death across my face.
So mysterious, so secret is your way
Restlessly I toss, and yearn for day.

Redecorating

You think this white upon my chin is skin.
It ain't. It's paint.
You think the spot on my skirt is paint.
It ain't. It's dirt.
And should there be about my eye
An azure blue you think is sky,
It ain't. It's dye.
You see, I've been fixing chairs and things
Removing paint with lye that stings
I'm so nearly dead I should have wings.
I ain't.

Rest In Peace

Sometimes, when the sun is bright,
More often in the dead of night,
I feel your presence in my room
And up my spine there runs a shiver.
Dead lover, is it you, or just my liver?

Your living body filled me with delight,
This ghostly shadow causes only fright
And, so I plead: Sweetheart, stay out of my room.
I'm fearful of cold, dead things that walk,
And if the neighbors knew, it might cause talk.

Poor Butterfly

Grasped in her small, warm hand
She brought you in, poor butterfly.
"See pretty paint upon its wing,
I shall get many and put them in a book."
I gave you one sad look, poor thing.

The child had never been held fast by circumstance
But I, imprisoned from the sunlight,
Grew heavyhearted at your plight.
Beautiful symbol of the Resurrection
Of our dear Christ who died.
'Tis hard to see you suffer, to see you crucified.
Poor butterfly.

Mother's Message

I had forgotten so much that you taught
And grown callous and hard with the years
Till I read your letter. The message it brought
Made my hard eyes grow tender with tears.

I could hear your dear voice, sweet and tender,
I could feel the cool touch of your hand.
Since you have died, do you still remember,
And remembering, can you understand?

Perhaps, you were thinking. Perhaps you remember
And that is why I found your old letter.
I feel you sent me this message,
That you want your boy to be better.

You said, "I am lonely. I miss you, my son.
Just drop me a line, won't you dear?
The lilacs are blooming. You love them, I know.
The blooms are quite heavy this year.

I put a big bunch 'neath your picture today.
Their fragrance affords me delight.
'Tis bedtime, sweet dreams, God keep you, my son.
My dearest, my darling, goodnight."

A Lovely Lady Died

Years ago, a young and lovely lady died.
Looking at her unlined face, I was not satisfied.
Too young she was to die; her life seemed gay.
'Twas then I saw her soft, white hands; crossed they lay.
Such tired hands I had never seen, nor have ever seen again.
With unbelieving eyes I looked; my soul was seared with pain.
Life had been kind, divinely kind, from this one to depart.
Those tired hands, such tired hands, had held a heavy heart.

Someday

Someday, this body weak and frail,
Will cease its weary, puny wail.
This crooked path will straighten out.
I'll know what Life is all about.
Perhaps I'll fly on golden wings,
Sure, I'll go places. I'll see things. Someday.

Remorse

Sometimes I take the washcloth of remorse
And scrub my soul with the soap of repentance.
Then I feel like a ship upon a chartless sea.
As the days go by and flyspecks of desire
And fingerprints of error once again becloud my soul
I find my way to peaceful shore,
Guided by sympathy and understanding.

Courage

I dreamed one night that I was a king
    And as I sat upon my throne
A beggar knelt before me with supplicating moan.
    His eyes were wet with tears. I said: "Begone!
If you can weep your grief is small.
    Move on! Move on!"

A soldier came with halting step
    His face was drawn and white
And as he knelt he winced from pain
    Yet his eyes were bravely bright.
"I came, my liege, with eager zest
    To tell you of a subtle jest."

"Rise, hero, rise. Ne'er kneel to me.
    You cloak your grief with mirth.
I kneel to thee, thou art a king,
    None greater on this earth."

Flowers For A Lovely Lady

A white rose and honeysuckle
Like the vine you trellised
To shield us from the side street.
Honeysuckle and a white rose:
I will not lay them at your feet.
They are not needed in your silver hair;
I shall lay them in the laces
At your throat, and fasten with
The old daguerreotype you like to wear.

Vocabulary

I always have definite reasons in my mind
Why I think this or don't think that.
But I'm at a loss to ever find
Words to express my reasons pat.
I resent it because of words I'm chary
And blame it on my vocabulary.

S. O. S.

I have ten little fingers,
I have ten little toes.
I have twenty little runners
Racing down my hose.
Really need a new pair,
Should buy them I suppose.
But where to get the money
The dear Lord, only, knows.

Just One More

One more illusion shattered.
It hadn't orter mattered
To have Jose go clickety clacket
Hunting son John's tennis racket.
But honestly—no fooling—
My eyes with tears are pooling,
Just one more god, from heights supernal,
Is busted. Jose has gone Maternal.

Loving a Man

A woman who loves a man wants to cook and sew,
To keep a budget, pay the bills, watch where the pennies go.
A woman who loves a man wants a child or two,
Wants them to have their daddy's eyes, be they brown or blue.
A woman who loves a man knows joy there's no transcending
And life holds for such a woman a very happy ending.

Obituary

Beautiful our love has been,
I would not soil its lovely sheen
With discord and dissension;
Thus, silently, we drift apart
With hurts too deep to mention.

About the Poet

As Josephine Barry Crump Trimble says in her foreword, generations of genes turned her into a poet. Her own mother, a brave Confederate heroine and later a prominent Methodist Church leader, published two volumes of poetry, *In The Ozarks* and *By The Fireside*.

From youth, Josie exhibited an artistic and literary bent and became a lover of prose and books. In maturity Josie was known for the twinkle of her perwinkle eyes, her ready and fresh wit, her compassion and sentimentality, and a rare ability to collect staunch friends, especially around the bridge table.

Born March 3, 1882 in Harrison, Arkansas, she was fortunate to have a devoted mother. Josie became the keenest observer of the vagaries of life, perhaps because of her own ordinarily devastating handicap. She was born with a scarlet birthmark that disfigured her left cheek. Instead of hiding, she grew up brave and created an especially outgoing and charming personality.

Josie in 1903 married Frank Glass, a Harrison pharmacist who died in 1904. leaving her with a small daughter, Josie Frank Glass. Two years later she married Guy L. Trimble, a former journalist who studied law with her father, Colonel George J. Crump and began practicing law in Harrison, where he later became mayor, 1919-22.

Guy and Josie had three sons, Guy Lee Jr., Vance Henry, and John Crump, and enjoyed an excellent life in Harrison until a violent railroad strike shattered family ties, and prompted Josie's family to move to Okemah, Oklahoma, where her husband became an oil boom lawyer.

Josie adjusted to a new prairie town, won respect for her intellect and charm. She directed a few community plays, fostered literary endeavors, and wrote holiday fiction for *The Okemah Daily Leader.*

In 1929, Guy Trimble moved his law practice and his family to nearby Wewoka, Oklahoma. There Josie repeated her successful entry as a newcomer. Most of her poems were written in Wewoka, during an extremely depressing period. Her daughter died in childbirth and Josie took two little granddaughters to raise. At the same time she was wracked by kidney stones, a painful malady that had begun in Okemah and became steadily worse.

The suffering did not daunt her. Her versifying pen [actually she preferred a pencil] was busy virtually daily. She helped organize the Wewoka Writers Club. Her scrapbook contains 200 entries, mostly delightful poems. She tried to cash in on jingle contests for the likes of Lucky Strike and Campbell Soups, but failed. Her beautiful poetry went mainly unvalidated. She did win a few awards in Oklahoma Writers Club competition. And published a small *Jittery Jingles* booklet for friends.

The Great Depression was cruel to many Oklahomans, especially the Trimbles. Guy, who bird-dogged likely oil leases, wrote that he was on the verge of a "great deal" that would enable him "to take mother" to the Mayo Clinic. The deal failed. Josie never had the advantage of any medical miracle.

Josie died in Wewoka on April 11, 1940, not knowing that just four days earlier Guy had died of uremia. They are buried next to each other in Wewoka's Oakwood Cemetery, under a stone that reads "Dear Hearts and Gentle People."

Finis

I want no marker placed upon my grave
Let literary oblivion o'er me sweep—
I long for rest.
My blasted hopes still grieve me,
Even in my sleep.

Text design	*Gail Carter*
Production consultant	*Patsy Willcox*
Book concept, editing and photography	*Vance Trimble*

PHOTOS

Front Jacket Elzene and Carol Ann, Houston, Texas, circa 1939

Back Jacket Elzene, Hermann Park, Houston Texas, circa 1941

Dedication Elzene, Galveston, Texas, April 23, 1939, on the beach with Carol Ann in bassinet beside Ford V-8 sedan

Bubbles Elzene and Carol Ann, Hermann Park, Houston, Texas, circa 1941

Dreams Elzene, Houston, Texas, June 8, 1940

Progeny Carol Ann and Elzene, Houston, Texas, December 25, 1940

Jittery Jingles Carol Ann and Elzene (behind the window) at 1620 Vermont Street, Houston, Texas, circa 1952

Yultide Carol Ann and Elzene, Houston, Texas, December 25, 1941

Memories Elzene, 1620 Vermont Street, Houston, Texas, circa 1953

Scrapbook Elzene, 3510 Woodbine Street, Chevy Chase, Md., circa, 1957

Shadows Elzene and Carol Ann, 1658 Danville Street, Houston, Texas, circa 1940

Poet Photo Josie Crump Trimble, Harrison, Arkansas, circa 1913. *Photo by Shattuck Studio*